LESSONS FROM THE ORCHARD

Speeding to my writing class
I killed a swallow.
No creation of mine
can redeem a bird.

LESSONS FROM THE ORCHARD

Diane Jackman

SACRED
EAGLE
PUBLISHING

First published in 2022 by Sacred Eagle Publishing Ltd.
The Chapters, Norwich NR15 2EB
www.sacredeaglepublishing.com

A CIP catalogue record for this book is available from the British
Library.

ISBN: 978-1-9999638-9-7

Typeset in Perpetua
Printed in the United Kingdom
Designed and Printed by Lavenham Press,
47 Water St, Lavenham, Sudbury CO10 9RN

CONTENTS   PAGE

Lessons from the Orchard

Threat of water

LESSONS FROM THE ORCHARD

Looking into the Little Orchard

The gate hangs in ruins.
I lay my hand on the wood,
eroded into striations,
as Gramp must have laid
his rough hand on the top rail
a thousand times past.

The Little Orchard, fruit trees
grubbed up long ago,
is choked with thistles
and rank hawkweeds.
Small creatures rustle and scurry
under the sheltering canopy.

I stand out in the kale field.
Here fifty years ago last January
I stood beneath the kale stalks,
their grey-green leaves
dripping ice on to my face,
soaking my pixie hood.

Then I thought this world,
this farm would go on forever;
calving, milking, sowing, harvesting,
on for as long as time. They would
have known, the grown-ups,
not clever, but full of knowledge.

When Gramp laid his hand
on the gate, he knew his action
had a finite number of repetitions,
might have been glad of the fact,
as the cold wind blew off the river
and shook the apple blossom.

Bottling peaches

Seven jars of peaches
gleam on the pantry shelves.
Half-globes of sun glow
slick with syrup, tempting,
perfect to my child's eye.

I watch my father slicing, stoning,
packing peaches gently with his strong hands;
into the range till the juices run.
A glance at the clock, the moment judged.
The iron door is opened.

> *Lift the loose glass lid.*
> *Pour in boiling water.*
> *Tap to release bubbles.*
> *Fit rubber seal.*
> *Replace glass lid.*
> *Screw down metal ring.*

Summer sweetness captured for Christmas.

When I find the peach tree
sheltered against the barn wall,
I stretch on tip-toe,
pick the lowest hanging fruit,
feel its furry bloom beneath my fingers.
I bite into the juicy flesh
down to the stone.
An earwig drops out.
I pick another and another.
Earwigs.

I hadn't noticed my father
crushing them under his broad thumb.

Pear Tree

In spring white blossom drops
bridal petals on our entwined limbs.

Such burning love runs its wildfire course
in summer heat, hectic, dries to tinder.

Damp winds of autumn shake down
a burden of ripening fruit.

In the grass a pear lies, flushed,
full-bodied, curving its promise.

Hollowed brown on the hidden side,
a last drunken wasp crawls out and stings.

How to catch a cricket ball

In the orchard, milking done,
we cousins played cricket with our Dads:
two stumps and a crooked stick,
a battered, but real, cricket ball
which any Test umpire would replace.
Hitting away into the plum trees,
the chicken huts, the ditch,
missing, because we knew
what was good for us,
the line of flapping sheets,
we finished with catching practice.

Uncle Guy had been to Oakham
and knew about cricket.
He threw the ball up straight and high,
shouted a name, gave us
time to run underneath it.
Cup your hands.
Draw the ball down
into your chest.
Now you're in control.
Stretching tentative and skinny arms
gave us only bruises and bent fingers.

We soon learned.

Swing

The nut trees stand
in a gnarled row, wind-whipped
and twisted into grotesque limbs,
as generations of labourers,
farming the tough land
since the Dissolution.

The Duke of Norfolk's spoils:
a distant scatter of houses,
of no account, no wealth,
no worth, almost no name.
Cotes. Cottages.
Could be anywhere. Nowhere.

> A hazel plat
> of Georgian pretension?
> Two rows of saplings
> unsold from the market garden?
> For me, the frame for my swing.

Binder twine and wood
salvaged from the tumbledown
pumphouse, thrown up to service
a wartime aerodrome.

A makeshift thing, dangling
crazily from a low branch.

No rough boys or bold girls
on the Rec. to steal my go.
Here I swung through summer days,
watched the green husks ripen
and harden into a handful
of nuts to feed a squirrel.

I think I'll grub up the hazels.
My tears were unstoppable.
Gramp wiped a weathered thumb
across my cheek and put
his mattock back in the barn.

The nut trees straggled on
in their scarecrow existence
until listed in the *Particulars of Sale*.

Nuttery:
An attractive plat of mature hazel.

Ninepence a pound

The week before you died
you spoke about the honey pears,
seeing them in the market,
one and threepence in wartime dearth;
how you told Gramp that night.
We've got an old honey pear tree
in the corner behind the Little Hut.

He picked a basket full,
walked two miles
up Nottingham Road
to the wholesaler.
Mr Vickers' eyes gleamed.
Bring me all you have.
Ninepence a pound.

The dray was loaded.
Wooden feed bins from the mill
covered the flat bed, brimming
with honey pears, hiding sweetness
and juice under russet patches,
turning to gold.
Enough money to buy a cow,

The first year the honey pear
had fruited
since taking on the farm.
And the last.

Annie Elizabeth

She brought the apple tree
on her marriage, a kind of dowry,
named for herself: Annie Elizabeth.

Tree: tall and upright in habit.
Fruit: crisp, very firm, a good keeper,
prominently ribbed and angular.

A tart description of my great-grandmother.

Her bridegroom planted the tree.
With her hands in the stone sink,
she could watch the purple-pink buds

open to a pale sheen of blossom
over-hanging the cattle trough,
where thirsty jostling cows

poached the land to a viscous mud.

The year I went to school
I saw my father falling slowly
through the laden branches,
the ladder sliding in the slurry
as he dropped into the holly bush.
My mother spoke, sour as a bitter-sharp.

She never was a woman to be relied on.

Annie Elizabeth - apple raised by Samuel Greatorex of Leicester 1857

The power of three

Three cousins picking blackberries
along the orchard hedge,
a harmonious picture, disguising

the stresses, the tension of three:
sister and brother, an only child.
In turn we learned to be the outsider.

Two girls, whispering secrets in the haystack,
refusing to climb down and join in
kicking the football against the cowshed wall.

Born within days in the same nursing-home,
an invisible bond forged, the quasi-twins
still conspired in childish pranks.

But when the chips were down,
parental fingers pointed, questions asked,
then *defend the tribe* was order of the day.

We didn't learn the power of three,
how three sticks are stronger than two
in holding up the sky.

The naming of flowers

As long as children learn the names of flowers
they will live to share the land.

I learned their country names,
the red and yellow of eggs and bacon
a more succulent mouthful
than bird's foot trefoil.

Daffodils with muddled petals,
sturdy natives on short stems,
coltsfoot, celandine and shepherd's purse;
violets in the dry ditch.

Stinking nanny, a puzzling name
for scentless mayweed; lady's smock
in a damp dell, bird's eye,
columbine and keck.

All white and lacy flowers were keck,
from cow parsley to hemlock.
All came with the warning
not to make a whistle from the stem.

Herb Robert, Jack-by-the-hedge,
Bobby's buttons and Aaron's rod,
Good King Henry, Lords and Ladies
danced through my dreams.

And now, if on the verge I see
a single poppy or dog-daisy,
yarrow, vetch or campion,
I am a girl again running through the orchard.

Envoi: Moon over the orchard

Damson black
the dark side of the moon,
pear silver fair her face,
pippin peel thin
the new moon rises,
swells to a golden plum,
ripe cherry red at full.

The moon cycles through the month,
tugs the young trees into growth,
draws from moon-pale blossom
the riches of orchard fruit.

The Shire Man

Tall and straight he stood.
For all his seventy years
He could still lay a hedge
Plough a straight furrow.
Craftsmanship they call it now;
To him a job of work,
A necessary skill.
From farm boy to farmer,
Pulled up by his bootstraps
He said to those near,
Not boasting, just describing
How it happened.

How many miles did he walk
Silent beside the horses?
Travelling the stallions
Carting from the fields.
Not many would do it today, he said,
Trudging along muddy lanes
To lonely farms and isolated villages.
It was his life
To be with heavy horses
His dearest wish
They should draw him to his grave.

Shire Horse Centre

Preserved in a museum
For my space age children
The artefacts of my childhood.
It was only my grandfather
Who hitched the heavy horses to the dray
Mended the swingle tree
Limped to the blacksmith.
Yet here they stand
Look look look look
Had he been eighty
He would have lived to know them both.
But time forces them apart
Into different worlds.

They cannot understand
And I, the bridge
Weep for the past
On the neat paved, teak seated playground.

A comparison of cows

Aberdeen Angus
neat, compact, black-suited,
serious faces, beady eyes,
Presbyterians, aware of their fate.

English Longhorn
old gals out on the lash,
variegated, scruffy, horns
going any whichway,
but eyes soft, doe-like,
up for a good time
before they die.

Winter Fields, Forncett St Peter

Straight ploughed furrows crumble
beneath the frost bite of the wintry storm
making all ready for Spring
and the sowing of wheat.

Beyond the whitening field
two skewbald ponies stand with nose to tail,
time-honoured, trap a blanket
of warmth between their flanks.

A rust red sea of cattle
crashes in the yard, surges to the rail.
They hear the farmer's boots step
hay-laden from the barn.

And here Dorothy Wordsworth
parted from the towering peaks of home
found quiet sanctuary
in the rectory meadows.

Names inscribed on manor roll
Burgess and Bartram, Howlett and Horne
still walk under the willows
beside the gentle Tas.

Common

Early sunset in November
at the hinge of the year.
Rooks straggle in untidy chains
across the darkening world.
Bare branches point beckoning fingers
to the sky. The rooks land,
clothing the ash trees in blackness.

Along the ditch primroses brave
the fickle blasts of March,
hugging the earth on short stems.
Luminous petals shine in the gloom
as if each flower can absorb
one scrap of fitful sun
to light the rumour of spring.

The cuckoo cries his summer warning.
An army of purple orchids
marches across the common,
welcome reinforcements each year.
Days grow longer, the grass grows tall.
The orchids are overrun,
mown down with the hay crop.

Hips and haws splash red in the hedges.
Plums and apples glow on twisted trees,
grown wild from the lost cottage,
its clay lump walls washed back
into the soil by years of autumn rain.
The leaves fall, bare branches beckon.
The rooks are flying home.

The path winds to the end

Ash twigs combed by March gales crack
and crumble in my path to the pond.
The meadow is still spongy,
waterlogged from a wet spring.

Mats of ground ivy breathe an acrid scent
of mint from leaves crushed underfoot.
They crowd out cowslips. Bluebells and
dog's mercury stand up to the invader.

A solitary bumblebee roams from flower to flower
its low hum drowned by the clatter of a passing train,
and the raucous chirk of a moorhen as she swims
across the pond to build her nest by the bank.

Hawthorn blossom fills the air with heavy musk.
Pale hawthorn leaves unfurl. The countryman's
"bread and cheese". They taste like
every other young greenstuff. No cheese.

Smooth leaves of teasels hide a prickly spine,
a portent of the spiky fruits of Autumn.
I startle a rabbit which flicks away. I cross
the ditch, below me a clump of matted fur and bone.

Twilight at Tivetshall Junction

A sickle moon hangs
over the disused goods line.

Bats fly from their roost
in a derelict engine shed.

From its perch on abandoned buffers
a thrush starts up its evensong.

Once alive with the sounds
and smells of poultry   cattle   coal
the yard lies sunken and split.

Rosebay willow herb   weld   yarrow
flourish in the pitted concrete.

Buddleia spikes spray unhindered
from the crumbling mortar
of a soot-black wall.

Docks scatter their rusty seeds
on the rising wind.

Stoneywell Cottage

Grandfather built this house,
growing from an outcrop of pre-Cambrian rock,
sinuous and organic,
fresh air for his wife's breathing.

Rooms with five walls,
offset staircase capped with slate,
a window at first floor to let in
children racing down the slope.

And his sons, raised in freedom,
and not to be outdone, built a fort,
heaved rock from the ground,
slow and painful work for young hands.

Every night, after dark,
Aunt Nell, stern and strait-laced,
slipped out unseen to add a few rocks
of her own, for encouragement.

His grandson lived there longest,
made a garden from the wilderness,
but still the house curves and carves
its natural way through the landscape.

He's eighty now, that grandson, and standing in the car park.

*Stoneywell Cottage is an Arts and Crafts house in Charnwood Forest,
built 1899 and now owned by The National Trust.*

Leaving Kangeq

The workers went first,
into processing factories,
once trawlers shovelled up the fish.
Wives and children followed.

With three families left,
the store ceased trading,
the priest was moved to a bigger parish,
the Government cut the power cable.

The name
of Kangeq
was rubbed out
of the record.

In the capital, new apartments
offered heat and light and water,
in a maze of concrete.
No one spoke our language.

Grandfather still dragged meat home
from market on his sled,
hauled it up three flights of stairs,
to the mocking laughter of our neighbours.

The sea was far, far from us.
Men who had been fierce hunters,
paddled their kayaks through ice floes,
found no place here, lost their way.

Chronicle

In this year
the man brings glass to the abbey.

It is made of sand and lime and ash, he says.
> *Yet light shines through.*

It was framed in the fire, he says.
> *Yet it is ice to touch.*

It flows and dribbles, he says.
> *Yet it is brittle.*

> He tears down the rough cloth,
> throws back the wooden shutters.
> He spreads the glass across space
> smoothes in the edges.

It will not rust or rot, he says.
It will keep out the north-easterlies.

> *Will it keep out the North-men?*

Song for a Fallen King

in 654 King Anna of the East Angles was defeated in battle and killed by Penda of Mercia at Bulcamp Wood near Blythburgh

The heron slowly beats its wings
Across the wide water,
Its cry an echo of the past
When harsher cries of stricken men
Resounded round the trees of Bulcamp Wood
And Anna fell to Penda's pagan arms.

The men who gladly took up arms
In widely sweeping wings
Besieged the pagans in the wood,
Drove them out towards the water.
Courage sang in the blood of Saxon men
To match the famous heroes of their past.

But swift the heathen horde swept past
By force of iron strong arms.
Fierce swordplay stole the lives of men
Who thought they flew on eagles' wings.
The blood of heroes stained the empty water
And ravens' cries resounded round the wood.

The ravening wolf prowled through the wood
Remembering from his past
No greater blood feast by the water.
He rent the bodies; legs and arms
Were torn off like a mayfly's fragile wings.
He gnawed the scattered limbs of shattered men.

Loud were the shouts of Penda's men
Amid the trackless wood.
The birds flew up on startled wings
As conquering Mercians trampled past.

They revelled in their fierce-fought clash of arms,
Their prize, the kingdom by the water.

Anna's kinsmen crossed the water
To pray for lifeless men.
His holy daughters raised their arms
In prayer for souls lost in the wood.
The glory of his kingship now is past
And Mercian pennants fly their raven wings.

Empty the water and the wood;
Gone the men into the past;
Broken the arms and folded the heron's wings.

Margaret Paston marries the heir

I have given my troth
and am come inland
to this red house –
captured by the depths of love,
locked four-square close
within a silent moat.
Only carp swim there
which this and every night
stare stiff from the platter.

My docile mare, wedding gift
from a loving husband,
steps safely through the quiet woods
beside the winding Wissey
where pigeons moan in the trees
and a kingfisher may light the willows.

But when the north-easter howls at dawn
and the wainscot shifts,
I am a girl again,
galloping Flint along the shore,
wind whipping through his loosened mane,
shingle hissing as the water slackens.
Gulls swoop and scream
and in the white-flecked sea
seal-heads come and go in the breakers.

As the sun comes up
I reach for my husband's arms
and am content
with love's captivity.

In the Reading Room

Here in the village reading room,
built by the bounty of Sir John,
I turn the pages of the *Chronicle*
in a half-light of guttering candles.
The world opens under my hands.

Foreign Intelligence small wars,
plague, revolution, toppled kings.
Cuttings from American Papers
murder on Chicago streets,
numbers of immigrants at New York,

maybe my daughter and her man.
Travellers' Tales lost in deserts,
frozen in snowfields, enchanted
by the flowers of Corsica.
Places I shall never see.

Carefully I fold the *Chronicle*, lay it
on the scrubbed table. Beyond the window,
the fields lie open under the moon.
Tomorrow I shall plough Lammas.
It is three-horse land.

How the Boar's Head Carol came to be

The Lord of the manor instructs his steward:
For the eve of Christ Mass
Get me a boar's head
With ivory tusks and golden bristles
Eyes gleaming emerald – or sapphire, I mind not.
In his noble mouth set an apple
Glowing crimson as Autumn woods,
Shining like the setting sun over the sea.

Surround his glorious head with bay,
The victor's crown, with sprigs of silver rosemary
And a garland green, leaves rich and lustrous.
At the nape and at the snout, three boughs of holly,
queen of winter trees with berries red
as blood-drops at his death,
All arrayed on a beaten silver charger.

Summon six singing boys
To escort him to the festive board.
Dress them in azure slashed with scarlet,
Each carrying a wax candle in a copper stick.
Let the dish be carried shoulder high
By a singing man with a deep and sonorous voice,
Fitting for the Lord's feast.

The Steward writes his shopping list:
one boar's head
with tusks
one costard apple
to fit
seven branches of bay
twenty sprigs of rosemary
greenery for the garland
three boughs of holly
blood red berries
six singing boys
one bass soloist
strong in arm and voice
one heavy silver dish
all for delivery
Christmas Eve
early.

Liberation Day
(Holland 1945)

Frozen in time
they sit on the bench
their backs to the cellar wall.
The wife, hands folded
leans against her husband's arm.
Grandma holds the baby.
Caught in the blast from our Sherman,
they sit for ever, contemplative, grey,
like the Leonardo cartoon.
In a moment of destruction we match
the artist's work of months.

THREAT OF WATER

The river is finally tamed
claim in an exhibition in Lee Valley Park Information Centre

Ley, Lyge, Leye, Lyzan, Lee.
My name changes from scribe to scribe.
Men try to capture me by words.
I am a shape-shifter.

Before the Romans came
I watered this land in season
flooded thirsty meadows to make
silt-rich grasses grow green.

Long forgotten are the water-gods.
The sword sacrifices, rusted darts
lie deep, dark-hidden from human eye.

For their puny trade men
cut through my banks. I am trammelled
by stone, funnelled in new courses
not of my own choosing.

My waters are shackled
in locks and navigations,
my flood confined and made safe
for a two-day playground.

The river is finally tamed.

Do not believe it.

Slow River

Through the overhanging alders
the sun throws a flickering newsreel
across the trunks of trees.

And the names of the dead are
written on the water-lily pads.

A banded argonis lands
on a broken reed and lifts
its wings to wait for the end
of its damsel-fly day.

Fading on the bank,
forget-me-nots.

Tea with Henry

Over his shoulder I watch
the Thames flowing by the café window.
Sunday afternoon figures stroll along the footpath.

Henry complains about the vulgarities of Palestrina.

The smooth surface of the water breaks into ripples;
choppy waves, choppy engine of a boat.
The River Police are making good speed.

The strip for the football tour of Tunisia is blue.

A knot of people on the riverbank
bend their bodies forward in alarm.
The police boat putters towards them.

They are painting the boarding house in puce and mustard, again.

A body is dragged from the river
and zipped into a white body bag.
No one attempts resuscitation.

Murray's sister, it seems, is fit.

A chill breeze blows in through the window.

Henry would like another Coke, please.

Across the river

budding trees beckon
branches fragment mysterious light
deceptive water

reveals the sandy bed
shrinking its true depth
I cannot wade

I cannot swim
I cannot interpret birdsong
cumbered

by the spent the wasted hours
- a spigot mortar lurks forgotten
across the river.

The reassurance of maps

He says the flats are built on the river,
actually *on* the river,
where the water can slipstream in secret,
a midnight feast on the foundations.

Their names bubble in streets and alleys.
Dallingflete and Cockey, Dalymond and Muspole.

The moss pool, surging out of the marsh
by St. Mary Coslany, seeking
blindly beneath the buildings
for the broader Wensum at Fye Bridge.

Stan is adamant. He has lived here
all his life. Not a man to be gainsaid.

I let him have his say for several weeks.
Until one day a neighbour speaks.
Stan frightens me. I lie in bed
and hear the walls creak.

And so the stream of untruth
must be dammed. I find a map.

The Muspole, culverted and contained,
trickles over St Mary's Plain,
winds along Muspole Street and runs
along Colegate to the waiting Wensum.

The flats are three streets away.

I show the map,
refute the fantasy.

Reassured they sleep easy.
Only Stan is damaged,
omniscience diminished
by the evidence of maps.

Incantation

Let down your hair, o watermother.
Let your waves spread over the land
filling the cracks and fissures
with the blessing of water.

Cradle your golden ball, o watermother.
Let your waves shade the sun
hiding its ceaseless fire
with the blessing of cloud.

Open your body, o watermother.
Let your waves break
in a fertile shower
with the blessing of life.

Watermother — bronze sculpture made by Fidelma Massey

Landward Cottage

The bedroom faced inland
No hotel sea view required
for fishermen. They wanted
a sight of dry land, children in the yard,
spread nets to mend.

That first night I lay wakeful,
the sound of waves rolling in
breaking at the foot of the cliff
different from city traffic, the sudden lulls,
moments of quiet when lights changed.

I began to fall into the rhythm,
counting the waves, listening
for the seventh, bigger, stronger.
My body began to move in concert,
imperceptibly, almost rocking

as each wave struck the foundations,
sunk deep into the cliff.
Not the granite of my Cornish childhood,
but sandstone, weak, fracturing
under the steady battery.

And I knew. Each day, each night,
as long as I lived here,
that relentless noise would play
the background music of my life.

It was the beginning of the desire to leave.

Lost Beach

When I went to my bed that night
I swear the beach was there
Shining silver under the moon
each grain of sand sparkling

Before dawn the wind rose,
howled down the chimney,
screaming like a banshee, like
Granny when a bat flew out of the coal shed.

And the beach where I used to walk
with my boys, and if no one was about
tuck up my skirts and paddle, letting
the waves tingle between my toes

Gone

Now I look out on a wasteland
of mud and jagged rocks.
Only ooze will tingle between my toes,
while the wind still moans.

I am at the end, lying on my last bed.
I can see the stretch of our lost beach
running down to the sea,
still an expanse of mud and rock.

They say the sand will come back.
One day. Not in my lifetime.
Midnight and the wind rises to a tempest,
howling down the chimney.

Before dawn I look out, see
grains of sand sparkling
under the fading moon.
I have waited long enough.

Last gravestone, All Saints' churchyard, Dunwich

Chewing daintily at every tide,
taking greedy gulps in winter storms,
the sea has swallowed this church, this town,
bite by bite and over centuries.

Jacob Forster: his name carved deep,
with space below for his Susannah.
Her name is absent, though her bones
may lie gently beside him, as in life.

Winter sun breaks through the sheltering elders
A robin flies down and perches on the stone.
Soon, Jacob and Susannah will wash over the cliff,
join their neighbours beneath the waves.

New Year at Morston

Barn of flint and brick
and broad planks,
substance, simplicity
for modern country living.
Empty stone-flagged rooms
for salt-stained boots
and wet dogs;

But down the lane
across the green
the saltmarsh lies
bare to the sky.
A shingle spit
protects the land.
For now.

Winter storms will
break through, rush
down the loke,
knock impatient
at the willow-green
double doors.
And they *will* come in.

Rain

We stop beneath the dripping trees
for another kiss.
Lifting my head to unaccustomed height
rain slides from your lion hair
into my nose,
and my breath is twice-stopped.
The gilt chain of a bag
too small for use
slips from my shoulder.
Cars pass showering water.

But these distractions
only cement the memory
of dark and lamplight and rain and love.

Mystery

I am an earthbound creature.
Air and water trouble me,
and yet the call of the sea is strong.
Cargo ships, bills of lading,
dwindling docks draw me
in polar inevitability.
Coffin ships, flags of convenience,
a fascination of words.
I read the *Derbyshire* saga
like a familiar dog-eared book,
I who never sailed a boat
nor learned to swim.
What salt-blooded ancestral veins
produced me?
Not the first Arthur Merton
who drowned at Jutland.
Plucked from the heart of a Midland shire
and pressed in time of war,
he tossed on the icy water
and sank.

Generations of farmers,
known by name,
stretch back to 1492.
Unless
a by-blow lurks among them,
learning to hide his webbed feet
in farm boots.

Mending shoes

With no money and no work
my hungry grandfather begged scraps
of leather to mend his family's shoes.

Two children lost, his broken heart
beat this refrain, survivors must
keep dry feet. In the cold kitchen

he lodged a shoe on to the last,
levered off the papery sole
and measured, fresh and fat, a new

sole from his hoard. Dreaming broken
by woodpecker taps, my father
woke to shoes, good as new, polished

bright by spit and rag,
ready to step out into
another cheerless day.

picnic on Beacon Hill

sports jacket
open neck
grey flannels
monochrome
curled snap-shot

on the trig. point
he stands easy
hands in pockets
adding more height
to Beacon Hill

a willowy youth
fair haired good-looking
before the army
takes him fattens him
up for total war

too soon he disappears
slips sideways out of time
his uncle still recalls
the Brownie box bought new
for idle summer days

Pre-Cambrian
indifferent
Beacon Hill
remains

Unremembered Woods

The names come from myth:
Pignut Spinney, warm and brown.
Hangingstone Rocks, black and carmine fissures.
The Outwoods, brilliant with bluebells.

My father rambled and scrambled
through trees and over rocks as a boy,
with Ernie Brewin of the crumpled ear.
His new mother spilt candlewax on his head.

My mother courted among the bluebells
dropped the flask of tea on a parched Sunday.
Not the only thing that made
the afternoon so memorable.

The children in our street
Are you coming up Hangingstone?
Bikes, Corona, sandwiches in greaseproof.
I was never allowed.

Sixty years on, from my distant home,
I've pinpointed the names on a map.
I shall go on pilgrimage before I die,
see for myself at last.

Musicians for dinner

Shut out by a five-barred gate,
runes of an ancient language,
obsessing, fulfilling my three companions,
I wash up and listen to *The Four Quartets.*

Structure, form, spirit,
shape, contour, architecture.
Words in parallel

Yet one is Greek to me,
the other the opening gate to understanding.

Love Song

When you die, I told him,
I shall go to Alexandria on a bicycle
with the insurance money.
An eccentric English lady
of the Agatha Christie school
with pith hat and veil,
I shall cycle to Luxor and Karnac,
a relict of the past.
Logistics, sand, heat, flies
do not feature in fantasy.

But when you die,
I shall be cut in half.
It will be hard to cycle
with only one leg.

Stones

Year 1
the stone was a red heart,
or not stone everything unreal then
brick washed into shape,
brick the makings of a house
once upon a time

Year 2
black stone flint jagged
edged and sharp to cut
new into the sea
not blunted yet
by endless waves

Year 3
grey and black banded
pillow stone
a deep incision
something missing
a lost life form fossilized

Year 4
tiny and grey
shrivelled remnant
smashed away
from solid rock
almost invisible

Year 5
pure
pearl white
shining
edges smoothed
self-contained

they line up on the windowsill
in the silent music room
gathering dust catching sunlight
as the mood takes

how many more must build the cairn
before we dance together?

Today

Today
the creamy roses
budded under African skies
touched by a finger of frost.
glowed gold against the grass

Today
I was tempted
to lie snug against you
and draw the green duvet
of warm earth over us.

But today
I must go home
and cook lunch
for the survivors.

Life story in eight sentences

One: infancy
house arrest on the farm
bounded by uncrossable roads

Two: school
eleven years hard labour
with time added on
for good behaviour

Three: university
open prison with six months
on the final treadmill
eat work sleep

Four: release into wage slavery
the single escape tunnel
lined with nappy buckets

Five: life sentence
with no remission
children

Six: solitary
the Governor transfers
your cell-mate to another place

Seven: sensory deprivation
deafness
glaucoma

Eight: suspended sentence
Alzheimer's
waiting

Building the wall

first you mix the days of the week
not so alarming

then morning and   evening   day and   night
    we don't mention the time

meanings of words   drift   away   baffling
                              abstractions
         talk is plain

familiar objects lose their names
                              pill
                                   chair
                                                       cat
              we point at things

other people   move   into the house   into our bed
       I am   me   and

          someone else

a simple event   becomes   a   tale

              toldinjumbleandcrash

your   doily   memory

                                        breeds   suspicion

              I am silent to avoid distress

When we met we laughed and laughed.
Sixty years to catch up, we told each other stories.
We'll never run out of conversation, we said,
When we're old and forgetful
We can tell the same stories over and over...

It has not been as we imagined,

building this wall.

Second thoughts

Following my heart I moved into town,
unmindful of the consequences.
Walls close in on every side.

I am envied for this house nestling
in the shadow of the church,
tucked away behind the market square.

But what is a short step to the baker
against a field, ploughed or grazed,
brown hens fossicking in the yard,

a walnut tree dropping red catkins
on the grass beneath bare toes, the sky
open, uncluttered to the horizon?

Swallow daughter

i.m. Eleanor Clare Jackman (1972-2020)

I missed the swallows this year;
their gathering on the wires,
chattering, preening, ready,
and one sudden morning, gone.

They must have been sitting,
as I sat beside you,
wires within holding you in life
ready for your final gift,

While you flew
away from us
beyond the horizon
with the swallows.

ACKNOWLEDGMENTS

Poems in this collection have appeared in:

Outposts, Grey Hen Press, Bangor Literary Journal, Poetry Space, The Norfolk Long Book, Little Ouse Press, Spillway (USA), Shot Glass (USA), WordsMyth, Chuffed Buff Books, Lettering Arts Trust and various competition anthologies.